KARATE
FOR BEGINNERS

KEITH VITALI & KENT MITCHELL

Contemporary Books, Inc.
Chicago

Library of Congress Cataloging in Publication Data

Vitali, Keith.
  Karate for beginners.

  Includes index.
  1. Karate.   I. Mitchell, Kent.   II. Title.
GV1114.3.V57   1983   796.8'153   83-10049
ISBN 0-8092-5531-6

Photography by Norman DeWalt

Published by Contemporary Books, Inc.
180 North Michigan Avenue, Chicago, Illinois 60601
Manufactured in the United States of America
Library of Congress Catalog Card Number: 83-10049
International Standard Book Number: 0-8092-5531-6

Published simultaneously in Canada by
Beaverbooks, Ltd.
195 Allstate Parkway
Valleywood Business Park
Markham, Ontario L3R 4T8
Canada

Contents

Foreword

Every sport has its superstars. They are the athletes who can run faster, throw harder, shoot better, and in the case of point karate, score more points than their peers.

Then there are the individuals among those superstars who have a little something that is even more special. They have the personality, the charisma, and the healthy ego that sets them apart from the crowd.

In karate there have been three such individuals to date: Chuck Norris, Bill Wallace, and Keith Vitali. Keith Vitali, like Norris and Wallace before him, has won every point karate title there has been to win. And in so doing he has won the hearts of karate competitors and fans everywhere that he has performed while winning the national point championship three years in a row. But his influence didn't stop in the ring.

Time and again Keith has proven his effectiveness in teaching as he motivated countless students to excel in competition. He has further impressed everyone in the media, from newspapers to television. He is a walking missionary for karate.

Vitali's next conquest is the silver screen. With the completion of *Revenge of the Ninja,* he has successfully communicated his great talent through a medium whose audience numbers in the hundreds of thousands at the very least.

It has been a great pleasure to know Keith Vitali. In these days, when superstars are commonplace, Keith still rates a cut above even the ordinary superstar. It is indeed refreshing to draw from his wealth of talent and to see one so gifted make such positive contributions.

Joe Corley
Executive Vice-President
Professional Karate Association

Preface

I decided to write this book because of the success I've enjoyed with my own students. And it is my hope that you can enjoy similar success—especially success comparable to that of the students at my Forest Park, Georgia, studio—by following the instructions outlined in *Karate for Beginners*.

I commissioned one of my black belts, Kent Mitchell, to help me write this book. He is a professional writer with 13 years of experience on the sports staff of *The Atlanta Journal-Constitution*. He also has 10 years of experience in karate.

During my years of worldwide competition I have been fortunate to have trained with some of the best karate men in this nation and abroad. One of the main traits all of them shared was the knowledge that the fundamentals were the most important part of their karate education. In this book I would like to share that, plus other things I've learned from them, along with my own experience.

Bear in mind that proper attitude is also important. Keep a positive outlook at all times during workouts.

Here is a special word of advice I always give to a student who wants to know how to improve his kicks or punches: If you want to be the best spaghetti eater in the world, do you run, jump rope, lift weights, or eat spaghetti? The answer is obvious. It follows, then, that if you want to be the best kicker in the world, you don't run, jump rope, or lift weights. You kick. Running, jumping rope, and lifting weights are helpful and have their place in karate, but the thing that makes the good kicker or puncher is kicking and punching. The key to excellence is repetition. The key to being a good kicker is to practice kicks over and over. Other things are good for conditioning, but you must work at kicking and punching above all else.

Acknowledgments

I would like to express my appreciation to Joe Corley and all the students at the Joe Corley Studios. A special thanks goes to the students at my Forest Park, Georgia, studio for their loyalty and support over the years, which means so much to me.

Individual thanks go to Stacey Duke, Jerry Prince, Eddie Jones, and Jeff Farmer for their assistance with the book's photography as well as their friendship. And thanks to Norman DeWalt for the photography and Tari Hoyt for her kind help.

A special thanks also goes to my friend and student, Kent Mitchell, who cowrote the book. Without his help, this wouldn't have been possible.

Keith Vitali

1

Getting Started

Today's karate students can, if they wish, live out their daydreams in the studio or at a tournament. They can, figuratively speaking, be dragon slayers, taking part in actual combat but without the risk of getting killed in the process. Saying that an evening of sparring in a studio or at a weekend tournament is exhilarating and satisfying is like saying that a drink of water to a thirsty man is "nice."

Karate was a mystery to most of us in the United States as few as 30 years ago. It began to grow quickly here, though, as more and more servicemen came home from the Far East with exciting new fighting skills and began to pass them on. It grew to huge proportions in the 1970s with the coming of Bruce Lee movies and the "Kung Fu" series on television. At one time it seemed as though there was a karate or kung fu studio on every block.

As will happen when there is a glut of anything, however, the bottom fell out of the karate market for a while. But this turned out to be for the best, because it weeded out many unscrupulous operators and weak schools, leaving for the most part a strong,

On the attack: Keith presses attack on Dave Smith during a team competition featuring Keith and his Atlanta Magnum Force.

solid base for growth. Today karate is growing again, partly because of the crime in the country, which presents a need for personal defense, and also thanks to the Professional Karate Association, which has weekly full-contact programs, carried on a national television network. Interest in this new type of fighting has been phenomenal and has helped point, or light contact, karate flourish. And it has attracted students whose simple wish is to be able to walk the streets without fear.

In addition to the fun and excitement of tournament karate and the sparring classes, the sport also provides a sound physical conditioning program second to none, and it offers a bonus no other sport can claim: you can take it off the playing area and into the streets where it remains a useful tool, not only for self-defense, but for self-confidence as well. One of the biggest pleasures of teaching karate comes from watching a student's self-esteem grow as he or she progresses month by month. This self-confidence carries over into daily life, and the individual is transformed into a new person.

Size and sex are not restrictions in karate. Anyone who wanted to be on the high school football or basketball team but was handicapped by size or refused admission because of sex will appreciate a sport that opens its doors to all. Age is no barrier, either. I know of more than one student who has taken the rigorous and difficult black belt examination after the age of 40 and come through it proud and intact.

It's a tough and demanding challenge, but anyone who makes up his mind to stick with karate can work his way to that almost mythical goal of black belt. You can spend as few as two hours a week or as many as 18 or 20, depending on your interest and time restrictions. Obviously, the more time you spend each week, the faster you will improve.

The space requirement is small (some Asians had to work out secretly in caves centuries ago, as knowledge of martial arts or owning weapons was outlawed). A basement, a garage, even the den or family room will do. Equipment isn't extensive for beginners—a uniform, a full-length mirror, a heavy body bag, and maybe some hand-held blocking shields if you have a partner to share your workout. You need the mirror to ensure that your form is correct, and the bags are to develop power.

For the first few months you will be working especially hard on flexibility, form, and focus. You never quit working on those three, but the first few months are critical. The best fighters are the ones who are well grounded in the basics, the fundamentals, and that's what this book contains, the basics of karate. It's a place to build from.

Here's a suggestion: set a goal before you try your first punch or kick and keep that goal foremost in your mind at all times. There will be times when you are ready to give up, because your stretches don't seem to be improving or your kicks or punches feel uncoordinated, but hang in there. It's a feeling every black belt has had. That goal will get you through the tough spots. Stick with it; you'll be glad you did.

Once you have a good feeling about the basics, you'll need to find a class or at least a teacher, because there are many fine points that students can't teach themselves. If you are uncertain about a school, contact the Professional Karate Association, which has a nationwide network of affiliated schools, for a recommendation.

Good luck, work hard, and have a good time.

2

Flexibility

A 270-pound pro football tackle requires enormous strength in his legs and upper body. A home run hitter in baseball must have strong wrists and arms. A champion sprinter needs extremely strong legs. Their bodies must also be flexible, and the karate fighter must be the most flexible of all.

It has been proven over and over that muscle flexibility is the key to warding off injuries such as pulled muscles. Many professional football, baseball, and basketball teams have full-time flexibility coaches today. But flexibility for the karate fighter is even more important, because flexibility is the lifeblood of karate. Without it you not only can't make the high, beautiful kicks; you also lose the critical element of speed. And without speed you have no power.

Beginning students should expect to spend a minimum of 15 minutes (more time is better) stretching before each class. The following exercises are the same ones used nightly at our studios.

Begin gradually by running in place for two minutes. Keep up a moderate pace and be sure to get the knees high—at least to waist

5

Kicks like this result from hours of stretching to improve the body's flexibility.

level. Running in place is followed by another two minutes of jumping jacks. These two exercises get the blood flowing, raise the body temperature, and get the muscles ready for the stretching to follow.

Next is head and neck rotation, 20 times in each direction, to loosen the neck and upper back muscles. It also allows you to get your breath from the opening exercises.

Shoulder shrugs, 20 forward and 20 backward, follow, and then full-circle swings of the arms, 20 in each direction.

Working downward, the next exercise is to loosen the muscles in the back and sides. Grasp one hand with the other directly in front of your chest muscles, spread your feet shoulder width apart, and twist your upper body to the left and right. Turn far enough so that you are looking over your shoulder directly to the rear. Do 20 of these to each side.

The next exercise is designed to loosen the muscles of the waist and hips, which is very important for kicking. Place your feet shoulder width apart and move your hips in wide circles while keeping your head and shoulders as still as possible. Imagine that you are trying to keep a hula hoop circling your waist.

To loosen the knees, put your feet together and bend your knees to a half-squat position, then bend over at the waist and place both hands on the knees. Now rotate the knees in small circles to the right for 20 counts and reverse the process when you finish. All this is in preparation for the stretching that comes next.

Place your feet shoulder width apart and bend your upper body forward at the waist as far as it will go (the objective is to bend your body almost double, so that your head is almost directly between your knees). Be careful to keep the upper body straight, not tucking the head down or bending the lower back, because this puts a strain on the lower back that could be harmful. Once you've bent down as far as possible, try to bend just a little more by holding onto your ankles and tugging gently. Don't yank or pull, just a gentle tug that will move you down a little bit. Here's a rule of thumb that goes with any stretching exercise: tug until you feel a slight burn in the muscle and hold. Count to 10 and straighten your upper body. Now bend down and repeat the exercise. From the same starting position, bend down and try to touch your head to your right knee. Hold for a count of 20 and repeat on the left side. Then bend forward again. This drill stretches the hamstring and lower back muscles. Now spread your legs farther apart and go through the drill once more. When you've done that, spread your legs as far apart as possible and repeat.

By this time your legs should be spread well apart, so the next

Bend the body forward from the waist, keeping the back straight.

Bend down and touch your head to your left knee, then repeat the stretch to the right knee.

Above: Bend one knee, while keeping the other leg straight, with the foot flat on the floor. Below: The key to this stretch is that the body is in an exaggerated runner's starting position, with the extended leg resting on the ball of the foot.

The American split is the objective of this series, but it might not happen on the first try.

exercise will follow naturally. With your feet still in place, turn your body to the right, swiveling your feet in the direction of your turn, and bend your right knee. Be sure that the rear foot remains on the floor, with the big toe, arch, and heel touching the floor. This position is for stretching the groin muscle. The more you bend your right knee and extend your left leg, the better. Hold this position for a count of 20, then turn in the opposite direction and repeat.

Now turn back to the right and this time rest your extended left leg on the ball of your foot with the heel pointing up as though you were on starting blocks. Again, the more you bend the right knee and stretch the left leg, the better. Keep your body as upright as possible during this stretch.

From the same position, turn your body so that your hips are facing forward again. As you turn, your right foot will swivel counterclockwise, and the toes of your left foot will point straight up, with that leg resting on your heel. Hold this position for a count of 20, then shift to the opposite side and repeat.

Once this exercise is complete, shift back to the first version. Bend your right knee; straighten your left leg, keeping the foot touching the floor with the toe, arch, heel alignment; and slowly slide that leg out as far as you can go. Now allow the right knee to unbend and slide the left leg even farther until the groin muscles won't allow you to stretch anymore. During this stretch, which is called the "American" split, you may use your hands on the floor to allow your body to go down slowly, avoiding a slip and painful injury. Don't be disappointed if you don't achieve the full split on the first try. Just keep working and the muscles and ligaments will finally stretch out. In my studios we include flexibility in our tests, and students must show improvement at each stage of their development.

Next comes the "Japanese" or "Russian" split. Facing the mirror, place your feet shoulder width apart and slowly begin to let them slide outward to each side, keeping your body upright and your feet flat on the floor, with your toes facing forward. Once your legs are as far apart as they will spread, bend down from the waist (keeping the back and neck straight) and try to touch your elbows to the floor. Do this for a count of 10 and then straighten your body from the waist up. Now try to spread your legs a little more and bend down from the waist again. Hold for another count of 10. Straighten from the waist up again and then bend to your left and try to touch your head to your left knee. Count to 10 and repeat the process on the right side.

Keeping the legs spread out, try once more to move them apart just a little farther, this time rotating your legs until the toes of

The "Japanese" or "Russian" split frees the groin muscles.

While in the Japanese split, lean to your side and try to touch your head to your knee, which will stretch the leg and side muscles.

Turn toward one knee and lean forward until your nose touches it. This helps the hamstring muscle.

both feet are pointing upward and your body is resting on your heels. After you've stretched to the limit, put one hand behind you and slowly ease yourself into a sitting position with your legs still spread. Be sure to keep your back straight when you sit and don't bend at the small of the back or bend the neck. From the sitting position, put your hands behind your head and lean forward as far as possible. Hold for a count of 10. Raise your upper body and then lean to your left and try to touch your knee with your head. Hold for a count of 10 and then repeat the exercise to the right side. Now try to slide your body forward a little more, but keep your heels in the same position. This will spread your legs farther. Repeat the bending exercises.

After the second set of repetitions, slowly move your legs until your feet are together. With your legs straight in front of you, pull your right foot toward you until the heel is as close to the groin as possible, the knee flat on the floor. Keeping your left leg flat on the floor, lean forward until your head touches the left

Above: Tuck one foot up as close to the groin as possible and lean forward until your head touches the knee. Below: With both legs straight ahead of you, lean slowly forward, trying to touch your head to your knees.

knee (hold on to your left ankle and tug gently to aid this exercise). Hold for a count of 10. Repeat this exercise with the left leg drawn in, then straighten both legs and try to touch your head to both knees. Be very careful doing this, tugging gently at the ankles. Don't hurry; it will happen in time. Hold for a count of 10 (as time goes on, extend the counts to a full minute).

These drills are preclass warm-ups and should be done before every workout. Never try to kick without stretching your legs (except in an emergency situation, when the adrenalin will take over). At this beginning point in your lessons the stretches are every bit as important as the kicks, and they will continue to be as your career advances.

3

The Punches

You've heard about karate punches, I'm sure. They're supposed to have almost supernatural power, if you believe what you have seen in movies and on television or read in books. There are stories about someone making his hands tough enough to penetrate wood or mortar, and many people wonder if it's worth the pain and torment. The modern-day American karate teacher will agree. In the days when those extreme hand-conditioning drills were used it wasn't unusual to have to punch through some kind of body armor. Today you can be almost 100 percent certain that the person you have to fight in the street won't be wearing body armor; therefore, there is less need to mangle your hands into condition.

The karate punch is still strong, but it is technique that makes it so.

THE STANCE

The punch begins with the stance, which is the foundation of all karate fighting. It is said that all the time you are fighting—

A good stance is a strong foundation for a good fighter.

punching or kicking—you are "chasing" your balance, or stance, as you have to work very hard to keep perfect balance in order to execute the next technique. The karate stance is designed to be perfectly balanced, so that the fighter can move in any direction— up and down as well as backward and forward and laterally. To find your stance, stand at attention, feet together, hands at your sides. Spread your feet to shoulder width, move the right foot back one step, and turn your body about 45 degrees to the right. To be sure that the rear foot is positioned properly, kneel—from the fighting stance—and touch your left heel with your right knee *without moving your right foot.* If you can touch your knee to

Draw a line on the floor, or put down a strip of tape, and put one foot on either side. Keep the knees bent and have the rear heel slightly off the floor. Hands must be kept in the ready position.

your heel, you have a pretty good basic stance and the feet are the proper distance apart. Once you've determined your stance, always keep your knees bent and your body low. This allows you to move or spring with no preliminary movements. Preliminary movements, better known as *telegraphing,* are messages informing your opponent in advance that you are about to attack. Eliminate them and your opponent is caught by surprise. Don't be surprised if the bent-knee position produces some aches and pains in muscles you didn't remember owning. It will pass in a few days.

Now that you have your lower body in order it is time to get the upper body set up. In the left-side forward stance that you are in, the left hand is used for the jab or to block punches and kicks on the beginner's level. The first is held at about chin level, approximately one foot in front of the face. The elbow touches the body lightly and protects the rib cage from kicks, while the fist and forearm are blocking punches and higher kicks. The right fist is held slightly in front and over the solar plexus, protecting this most important part of your body and putting your fist in a good position to punch. Be sure that your right elbow is lightly touching your body just above the hip. Let the elbow point straight down and slide easily along the side. This protects the right rib cage and also trains your elbow not to flail wildly on punches.

Moving in the stance is quite comfortable once you get used to it. To move forward, move your right leg forward (maintaining the bent-knee stance) until the heel of the right foot moves just past the toes of the left, then slide the left foot forward until you regain the left-side forward fighting stance once more. To move backward, slide the left foot to the rear until the heel is even with the right toe, then slide the right foot back. Never touch the heel and toe together. Each foot should be moving along a parallel track, not one behind the other.

THE JAB

Now that you have your stance and can move with it, you are ready for punching. The first punch is called the jab. Since you are in a left-side forward stance, the jab will be done with the left hand, because you jab with the forward fist. The first two knuckles nearest the thumb make up the striking area, or weapon, of the jab. These knuckles are aimed at a target on the face or head (the jab is rarely used as a body punch because it lacks sufficient power), and the weapon moves in a *straight* line to the target. It returns along the same line on recoil. As the fist goes out it is

A

(A) Make a proper fist by holding the hand with the fingers pointing straight up. **(B)** Bend the fingers at the first two knuckles tightly, roll the fist up **(C)**, and tuck the thumb **(D)**.

B

C

D

vertical, but when it gets about three-fourths of the way to the target you turn it over so that it is in a horizontal position as it strikes. Power is derived by the speed of the technique. Therefore, emphasis should be placed on the recoil of the jab. Another method of delivering the jab is to twist your hip to the left and pivot your front foot in a clockwise motion at the same time that the arm is nearly fully extended. The combination of turn, twist, and pivot gives the jab considerably more power than simply popping it out and back on arm power alone. You throw the body weight with the jab.

A variation of the jab, and a weapon proven to connect, is the slide-up jab. Remember how you move forward in your stance? Execute a jab and move—step forward—with the punch. This closes your distance from the opponent, but he isn't able to reach quickly because he is watching your front foot to detect forward movement, and it stays put. Remember this: the weapon (fist) always moves first, and the body follows.

THIS IS A FIST

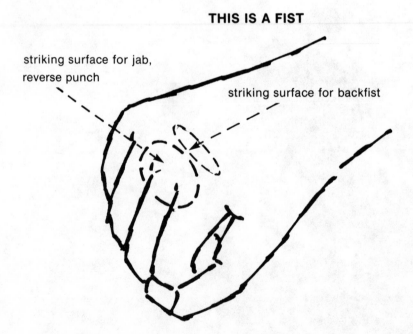

striking surface for jab, reverse punch

striking surface for backfist

THE BACKFIST

The backfist, like the jab, is executed with the forward fist. Like the jab, the backfist uses the two large knuckles as its weapons, but this time the hitting surface is the back of the knuckle. The execution is slightly different in that you simply send the two back knuckles directly to the target in a straight line, make contact, and return the weapon along the same line. Don't extend the arm fully on this punch, because it might hyperextend the tendons of the elbow. The backfist is a more powerful punch than the jab, and with it, a fighter can deliver a knockout blow.

THE REVERSE PUNCH

The reverse punch might be the strongest punch in karate. With it you can quickly learn to break a one-inch pine board from as short a distance as three inches. It is simply a matter of technique, which will make your weapon (the two forward knuckles) weigh as much as your body. This weight, plus the speed of the punch, makes it devastating. It is called the reverse punch because the hip is reversed from the normal stance when the punch is complete. No matter which side is forward, the punch is delivered from the rear fist, the one covering the solar plexus. To punch high, move your weapon in a straight line from its starting point to the target, the upper lip of the opponent. Like the jab, the fist is vertical until it is three-fourths of the way to the target. Then you turn it over, and as the arm reaches full extension (keep it slightly bent to avoid strain), twist your hips and pivot your rear foot. Remember, the hips turn at the end of the punch. The turn, twist, and pivot put your full body weight behind the punch. It's a matter of physics: force equals mass times acceleration. Using the karate technique, the mass of your fist increases from about 15 pounds to the weight of your body. The more mass, the more force. Then, when you build up speed, it moves into the realm of deadly force. Here's a clue for gaining speed: relax. Don't make a tight fist while you are waiting to punch or when the punch is on the way. Clench your fist at the moment of impact. Tense muscles

Start in the fighting stance.   Move the weapon first.

Then twist the hip and pivot the rear foot.

Note the fist position for the high reverse punch.

create a terrific drag on the body. The more relaxed you are, the faster you will be. Make yourself relax by constantly telling yourself to relax until it becomes habit and you find yourself relaxed at all times.

The next version of the reverse punch requires careful attention because of the difference in delivery. When punching to the body, and the reverse punch is your main body punch, the fist remains vertical instead of turning over. This is because in that position the physical makeup of the arm makes the punch stronger by keeping the fist vertical. As in the high punch, the weapon starts first, and when it is almost fully extended the hips twist and the foot pivots. In any kind of punch, be sure that you attempt to

Note the fist position is vertical for the middle reverse punch.

recoil it as fast as or faster than you send it out. This makes the fist go out faster and is another method of increasing punch speed. Remember, the weapon moves first.

To practice these punches, and you will need to drill constantly, stand before a full-length mirror and punch at your own image. Twenty punches from each side is good for starters. Remember, keep your whole body relaxed. Don't lean forward as you punch, because this puts your head closer to the opponent. Instead, use the hip twist and foot pivot to extend the punches. And always maintain the bent-knee stance, keeping the body as low as possible.

4

The Kicks

The high, graceful, powerful kicks are what make karate different from other martial arts. The kicks we teach in American karate are refined to fit Americans. They are also the ones that have been proven effective in hundreds of situations, in both self-defense and tournaments.

The legs are longer and stronger than the arms, and adding them to a fighter's arsenal gives him double the fire power of most of his adversaries. In competition with other karate students, though, it's a different matter. There, technique and fundamentals will make a big difference. The more fundamentally sound fighter nearly always has the upper hand. In learning the kicks in this chapter, it is important to remember that you will first be working for good form, then for power, and for speed after that. Good power and speed follow good form.

Four kicks, plus some variations, will be taught in this chapter. They are the building blocks for other, more sophisticated kicks, but by themselves they carry even a black belt a long way.

The kicks are what makes karate different from and more effective than normal fighting.

THE FRONT KICK

The name aptly describes this kick, which is delivered forthrightly to the front of the fighter in a thrusting motion. Generally it is used on the opponent's midsection in tournaments and the midsection and groin in combat. It is a kick designed to wear an opponent down, break the ribs, or put the opponent out with one shot if he is hit in the right place.

The weapon for the front kick is the ball of the foot. When the kick is executed, think only of sending the ball of the foot, not the

Start with the knee raised to position at least waist high.

Thrust the weapon (note the foot
position) straight at the target.

Then recoil back to the raised-
knee position.

Left: Looking at yourself in the mirror, your knee should be this high.

Above: Your weapon should look like this when extended.

Above, right: Always return the kick to the knee-high position.

entire leg, at the target. The best way to teach a front kick, and all other kicks as well, is in slow motion to a count of four.

Get into a front fighting stance, left side forward. On the count of one, raise your right knee to at least waist level, higher if possible. The supporting leg should be perpendicular to the floor, and the foot should be cocked so that it is pointing toward the floor with the toes curled back (otherwise, they'll break when they hit something). On the count of two, slowly thrust the weapon in a straight line to the target directly in front of you and hold it there. On three, recoil the weapon to the number one position. On four, the foot goes back to the left-side forward stance.

Practice the kick this way four or five times each workout, then execute the kick in one count. Do this at least 10 times on each leg.

Another version of the front kick is the front snap kick. The basic difference is that the weapon is delivered in a snapping, instead of thrusting, motion. It is a quicker kick and works well in combination with punches and other kicks.

THE BACK KICK

Sometimes called the *turning side kick,* this is another thrusting kick, but the heel is the weapon this time. To make the weapon, cock the foot tightly so that the foot and toes are curled up as tightly as possible in the direction of the shin. From this position, try to stomp on the floor directly beside your other foot, using only the heel. If you can do this without any other part of your foot touching, you have the correct foot position.

Now get into a left-side forward side stance, which means both feet are on line toward the target. On the count of one, rotate your shoulders and head and pivot your foot in a clockwise direction until your back is toward the target and you are looking at the target over your right shoulder. On the count of two, lift your knee as though you are trying to touch it to your right shoulder, which will produce an image in the mirror showing your heel beside your buttock, with very little of the leg showing. On three, send the knee in a straight line to the target and hold.

Practice the front kick for power.

Be sure to get the knee high so that the kick will thrust straight ahead.

Aim at the center of the target and try to kick through the pad.

The side stance as you will see it in the mirror.

The first move of the back kick is to turn your head and body.

Then pivot your feet but keep your back to the target.

Raise the knee and aim
the heel at the target.

The   completed   kick
should look like this in
the mirror.

The back kick as seen from the side.

Note how the heel is aimed at the target and how Keith's body is tucked as much as possible.

The kick itself. The heel is the most forward point of the kick. Notice that the toes are lower than the foot.

On four, return the weapon along the same line to the cocked, or channeled, position. On five, return to the side stance.

This kick is much easier when done in one motion, but the slow motion by the counting technique also teaches you the dynamics of the kick and builds up the kicking muscles as well. It is another form of isometrics. When doing the kick in one motion, be sure that the eyes are on the target before the kick is launched; otherwise you can miss the target and possibly injure your knee.

THE SIDE KICK

This is my favorite kick, and it is possibly the best one in the arsenal because it has so many variations and uses. We teach two versions to beginning students. As with the other kicks, both are taught first in slow motion, by the counting technique.

Face the mirror left side forward, and on the count of one, slide the rear foot up to the front foot. As the foot moves forward, turn it so that the toes are pointing to the rear in the opposite

The side kick starts from
the side stance.

Slide the rear foot up to the front foot and turn the rear foot so that the toes point to the rear.

Raise the knee and cock the foot so that the heel and buttocks are side by side in the mirror.

When the kick is fully extended you will see an image that looks like this. Note the difference in the foot position here and the position of the foot in the lower photo on page 39.

direction of the target. On count two, raise the left knee up in the same manner as you did in the back kick, as though you are trying to touch the knee to the right shoulder. This will cause your heel to point at the target. The image you should have in the mirror here is the same as the back kick—a heel directly beside the buttocks. On count three, send the weapon straight at the target, turning the hip over as the leg extends fully. In this position the heel should be blotting out the buttocks in the mirror. On four, return the heel along the same line, and on five, return to the side stance. It is important to keep the upper body as relaxed as possible during the kick, and try to lean no more than 45 degrees from upright; otherwise you can't follow up the kick with punches.

To execute the side kick in one count, slide the rear foot up, and as soon as it stops, raise the knee, kick, recoil, and return to the side stance in one motion. It will take much practice to get this kick to the point that it is an effective weapon. Try to get in at least a minimal amount of kicks each day at home.

After a few weeks you need to know a more advanced version of the kick. This eliminates one step and also helps you disguise the kick so that the opponent can't readily prepare a defense against a specific kick. The main difference is in the second and third counts of the five-part slow-motion sequence. Face the mirror left side forward and slide the rear foot up to the heel as before. This time, though, when you raise your knee, put the heel on a line with the elbow, shoulder, and head in the mirror. This means the knee won't be channeled as deeply as in the first version. On count three, send the kick out to the target. As you have noticed, the hip isn't turned over nearly as much as it was for the first version, and here is the second big difference: you must turn the hip over as the kick hits. This turning over of the hip is what gives the kick its power. On any side kick you must turn the hip to create this power. On four, recoil and turn your hip back, so that the body alignment is correct in the mirror. On five, return to the side stance.

THE ROUNDHOUSE KICK

This is the first slashing kick you learn as a beginner. It is a kick that also has many uses. One version is a power kick; another is to the feet what the jab is to the hands.

The first version we teach is the slide-up roundhouse kick. Face the target left side forward in a fighting stance. On count one, slide the rear foot up to the heel of the left foot, just like you did with the sidekick. On count two, lift the knee up in line with the target (or so that the kneecap is pointing directly at the target), so that the weapon, the instep, is at a 90-degree angle to the target. On count three, move the weapon to the target, keeping

Power practice with the side kick.

Note the position of the foot farthest away from the target as it slides up.

Raise the knee and cock the heel so that it is aimed at the target.

Try to kick through the target and recoil as quickly as possible.

In the roundhouse kick the knee is pointed at the target and the lower leg is at a 90-degree angle to the upper leg.

The weapon swings in a slashing motion to the target.

The roundhouse kick from the side.

Below: In this view the weapon is the ball of the foot, but the kick is the same.

Side view of the powerful back-leg roundhouse kick.

The cocked position.

The weapon (the instep here) slashes into the target and the hip turns over as the supporting foot pivots.

the knee in line with the target. It is simply a matter of moving the lower leg and keeping the upper leg stationary. On count four, return the weapon to the number two position. Go back to the fighting stance on count five. Be sure to concentrate on keeping the upper body as upright and relaxed as possible. The one-count execution of this kick is much easier than slow motion. Slide up, raise your knee, kick, recoil, and return to the fighting position.

The power version of the roundhouse kick is called the *back-leg roundhouse*. Instead of sliding up and hitting with the instep of the front foot, you use your rear leg, and the weapon is the ball of the foot.

But to start with, line up in the same position as you did for the slide-up kick. Again, slide your rear foot up to the front foot and again raise your knee on count two. This time, however, the knee is at a 45-degree angle to the target. The weapon and the lower leg are at a 90-degree angle to the upper leg. On count three, move the weapon toward the target. At the same time that the weapon moves, the knee will follow. But be sure that the knee doesn't go past the target. As with the first version, return to the cocked position on count four and to the fighting stance on count five.

Now you are ready for the back-leg roundhouse kick. From a left-side forward stance, simply turn your left foot as far as it will go to the left on count one. On count two, pick up your right knee and hold it at a 45-degree angle to the target with your knee bent at a 90-degree angle. On count three, two things happen almost simultaneously: you will move your foot to the target and turn your hip over. Turning the hip over is what provides the power of the back-leg roundhouse kick. To turn the hip over, you have to pivot your supporting foot as the hip is twisted. The final position in the mirror will have your supporting foot pointing in the opposite direction of the kick. Count four brings the weapon back to the cocked position of count two, and you return to the fighting stance on count five. The one-count version is one motion. The supporting foot is turning as the knee is raised, the hip is turning over, and the supporting foot is pivoting as the kick is going toward the target. Be sure to recoil quickly. The quicker the recoil, the faster the kick.

It will take constant work to make these kicks potent. You will have to spend hours working out before you are ready to kick with speed, power and focus.

One rule to follow as you work out and progress is to ask yourself these three questions: (1) Do I kick fast enough? (2) Do I kick high enough? (3) Do I kick hard enough?

If the answer to the first question is no, then kicking drills to the air in front of the mirror, emphasizing the recoil, will be the plan to adopt. Snap back the kick as quickly as possible. The common belief is that you are either born with speed or you aren't, but you are able to increase raw speed with proper practice. If the answer is no to number two, then additional flexibility drills are in order. High kicks might not be everyone's goal, but good flexibility increases your range and also increases speed and power in your kicks. If the answer to number three is no, then striking tangible objects is the key. Work with the heavy bag or striking bags held by a partner to increase your kicking strength.

5

Additional Training Information

The key to being a good karate fighter is to practice the art and seek perfection. You might never be perfect, but don't settle for doing "the best I can," because we all have a tendency to be easy on ourselves, especially when we are doing something that requires extra effort. The first few weeks of karate will produce some unpleasant feeling in muscles and tendons that haven't been used before. You have to push through this and keep going.

A good hour's workout will include all of the stretches in Chapter 2, plus several facets of Chapters 3 and 4. You might not have time to practice every kick and punch, but that's okay. Plan your workouts ahead of time and make them vary so that they won't get boring in a week's time. You might work on punches one day, kicks the next, and try some combinations of the two on other days.

There are other ways to get around what could become a boring routine. Jumping rope builds stamina and agility and is a good alternative to running in place and doing jumping jacks at the beginning of a workout. There are several kinds of jump ropes, ranging in price from the rawhide professional version that has handles with ball bearings to a simple plastic model. One good method for jumping rope is to do rounds of three minutes, with one minute's rest in between rounds. Don't try more than three rounds to begin with and don't be discouraged by your lack of physical grace in the beginning. We all go through that before we begin to get a feel for the timing. One good way to pass time while jumping rope is to play some music while you jump. In fact, music will enhance the mood of the entire workout. A good way to keep track of rounds, by the way, is with a simple egg timer. Then you don't have to watch the clock, which really makes a three-minute round last about three hours.

Sit-ups, plus any other exercises for the abdominal muscles that you can discover, are a must. The midsection must be tough to absorb punishment from kicks and punches. Many karate practitioners also believe that the midsection is the center of power of the entire body. Never do sit-ups with your legs stretched out straight on the floor, because this kind of sit-up puts too much strain on the lower back. One good way is to lie on your back, knees bent, with your feet flat on the floor, which puts about 75 percent of the effort on the abdominal muscles. Another way is to lie on your back and lift your head and legs off the floor. As you raise your upper body, the knees come back and meet the head at the midpoint. (Don't let the head or legs touch the floor once the exercise has started. This puts effort on both the upper and lower abdominal muscles.) Start with 25 repetitions of each and work up to 100.

There are two types of kicking drills—speed and power. You work on speed by kicking into air at your image in the mirror or at a partner. Power drills are done at a heavy kick bag or blocking shields held by a partner. You need both, because speed leads to power, and power leads to stamina and strength. You need all three. The first time you kick a bag with full power you'll understand the need for all that practice involving form and focus. If you deliver a kick and your weapon hits the side of the bag, making you fly backward instead of making you feel that satisfying sensation of a weapon sinking deeply into the center of the target, you know for sure that your form and focus are off. Power kicking requires great concentration, or focus, as well as great stamina. You should try to get in at least 15 kicks on each leg of each type of kick for starters and work upward. It will be tiring and frustrating at first, but once you begin making good contact you seem to disregard the fatigue.

Running is important, because it builds overall stamina and conditions the legs, which are very important in karate. Begin with a slow mile and add distance as your body dictates.

Push-ups are important and should be done on the two striking knuckles of each hand rather than the usual way on the flat palms. This puts strength in the wrists as well as the arms. Start with 25 and work up. Remember, push-ups are only as good as the form used in doing them. Keep the body straight, slowly let yourself down, touch your nose, and push back up. Don't bend your back on the way down.

Diet? Bill Wallace subsists mainly on McDonald hamburgers, plain, and did when he was the unbeaten Professional Karate Association world middleweight champion. Wallace is still a legend because of his lightning-fast roundhouse kicks. But to be careful you should try to maintain a balanced diet with plenty of fresh vegetables as well as meat, poultry, and fish. Diet is a personal thing, and each individual has different needs. As you progress in karate, though, you will become much more aware of your body's needs and physical conditioning in general.

It's a long trip from white belt to black belt, and every step can be fun. Enjoy yourself and work hard.

6

A Look at Keith Vitali

While we were still in the process of planning this book our editor suggested that Keith devote a chapter to telling about his rise to become the nation's number one karate fighter for three straight years—a feat only one other fighter, Bill "Superfoot" Wallace, has duplicated. He tried to do so but ran into a problem; Keith is one of those truly modest people who can't write about himself. So, it became my opportunity and privilege to relate the story of Keith's rise to karate fame.

First of all, let's understand that Keith's entire karate career hasn't been made up of winning tournaments, traveling all over the country, and hobnobbing with the top talent in the sport. In fact, it took this future national champion a full year to rise above white belt!

"I was studying under a Korean named John Roper at the University of South Carolina in Columbia," Keith said. "John made sure I had a very strong foundation. He took the time with me to make sure I had a good side kick, stances, and punches. With such a foundation, the rest came easy."

Keith connects with a Round Kick to the head of Californian Steve Fisher.

He's not exaggerating. After taking an entire year to reach white belt, it took only one more year for Keith to become a black belt, an accomplishment that comes close to that of Joe Lewis, who earned his black belt in a mere seven months. Both athletes, of course, turned out to be extraordinary.

Keith's tournament career progressed about as quickly as his

Keith attacks his old nemesis and good friend—Bobby Tucker.

early karate efforts. "I competed in my first tournament after two weeks in karate and lost," he said. Two years later, he lost his first fight as a black belt, too. And he fared no better the next week, again losing his fight.

"I thought it was over for me," Keith said. "Then I found out that I had lost against the number one fighter in the South. I didn't know it at the time I was fighting him, and I thought I should have won. I thought I was better than him, so when I found out, I realized I had some potential. After that, I got motivated, started working out, and won my next tournament."

Striving for the number one spot in his region was a slow but

Some of the "Carolina Mafia" (left to right): Mike Genova, Keith, Richard Jackson, and Bobby Tucker.

steady climb at first. Time and again Keith encountered one major stumbling block—Bobby Tucker. He lost to Tucker the first eight times he fought the fellow South Carolinian, who became a close and respected friend.

"*I* still think he's the fastest opponent I ever fought," Keith said. But while Tucker was winning, Keith was thinking, and the man who became known as karate's most analytical fighter won the next 10 straight confrontations with Tucker. There is some speculation that, if Tucker had been able to continue his dominance of Keith, he would have been the nation's number one fighter.

Man among men: Keith (center) with Chuck Norris and Joe Corley (right) after winning Battle of Atlanta.

While still on the rise in the South, Keith had his eyes set on being the nation's number one fighter. He idolized such fighters as Joe Lewis, Bill Wallace, and Chuck Norris and wanted to follow in their footsteps, but a not-so-funny thing happened on the way to the top—tournament karate went into a deep depression. Unlike the economic problems of our nation, the cause of tournament karate's decline was easy to pinpoint—full-contact karate.

In September of 1974 an event took place that almost wrecked tournament karate for good. The biggest names in the sport—Lewis, Wallace, and Jeff Smith, to name a few—gathered at the

Keith goes airborne to score a point on Bobby Tucker.

Los Angeles Sports Arena to compete for the World Professional Karate Championships. This was not just another tournament with an ambitious name; this was the launching pad for the Professional Karate Association of today. It was one of those special nights. There was an electric current running through the crowd that contained more celebrities than you could name, such as Telly Savalas, Ryan O'Neal, David Carradine, George Peppard, Peter Graves, Peter Fonda, and others. The judges were legends themselves: Jim Harrison, Takayuki Mikami, John Natividad, Joe Corley, Chuck Norris, Glenn Keeney, Pat Johnson. And then there were the fighters.

It was the place to be that night. If only those who won championships had stayed in full-contact while the rest left, tournament karate still would have been gutted. But a huge crowd lined up behind each champion, and none of them were thinking about point karate anymore.

Some eight months later the fight between Wallace and Joe Corley for the middleweight title in Atlanta's Omni put the black border on tournament karate's funeral notice. Wallace beat Corley before a crowd of 10,000. No one had ever before drawn that many fans to *watch* a karate fight. The enormous potential of the sport became instantly apparent. It was too much to pass up.

During this period Keith kept fighting in local tournaments, teaching and working out in full-contact as well. By 1977 he had established himself as the man to beat in the South, being named number one in both point fighting and full-contact in his region. He was also named one of the nation's 10 best fighters by *Karate Illustrated* magazine. The listing was alphabetical, so Keith was close to the bottom, but the magazine emphasized that it considered all the fighters on an equal basis. Some of Keith's students during this time were also rated highly regionally and eventually went on to national acclaim: Richard Jackson, who worked his way up to U.S. champion in the PKA's super-lightweight division in full-contact; John Orck; Tony Bell; Mike Goldman; and Keith's brother, Steve, who was a tough tournament competitor when he could get away from his Marine Corps force recon unit to compete. Keith also spent a lot of time at Mike Genova's studio in Columbia, working on new techniques with his tournament companion, which he would take back to his own students at the University of South Carolina.

By this time Keith had attracted the attention of Joe Corley, who had since retired from competition to devote himself entirely to the growth of full-contact, the Professional Karate Association in particular. Corley invited Keith to move to Atlanta and be chief instructor of his studio chain there. It would give Keith an opportunity to improve his income and pursue a career as a fighter as well.

"At that time I had to make the decision to fight full-contact or tournament," Keith said. "We both thought the smart approach was to focus most of my energy in one path: either be the best in full-contact or the best in points, because it was too much to divide. It panned out." Keith laughed, "With Benny Urquidez as one of my next fights, I thought it might be smart to hit the point trail. I enjoyed traveling, meeting people, and I could do that at point tournaments. In full-contact you fight once a month at the most. In point tournaments you can fight once a week, even two times."

And there was the training. If you aren't fighting, you have to be training all the time in full-contact. You not only have to work on your kicks and punches; you also have to work on taking the other guy's kicks and punches. It's time-consuming and would take too much away from a now-thriving studio and some very promising young students. Keith thought the price was too high to pay. Luckily for point karate, he left full-contact behind.

With Corley, Keith plotted out a strategy for winning the national title in 1978.

"After Wallace, Lewis, and other top fighters turned to full-contact there was a void on the tournament scene," Keith said. "I thought it was time to generate some interest again, so along with Joe Corley and some other promoters, we formulated a circuit, and from that came national competitors. The tournament circuit was quite new at the time; in fact, it wasn't in existence. The Mid-Americas (Minneapolis) was just having its first Diamond Ring Nationals, and Roy Kurban's tournament was just turning A-rated because it was attracting outside competition, but there were few A-rated tournaments at the time.

"I had been number one in the South in 1977 but had never been out of my region. Neither had any of the other nine fighters (picked by *Karate Illustrated*). I called up John Worley (in Minneapolis) and told him I would like to fight out of my region. He said, 'Excellent. Let's go ahead and maybe try to start up a circuit again.' We discussed it—that tournament means a lot to me even now—how we would be good for each other. From his tournament I got national prominence in the magazines for winning an A-rated tournament, and yet that tournament wasn't A-rated

The South East Karate Association Team (left to right): Dave Deaton, Keith, Joe Corley, Mike Genova, Larry Kelley, Tony Bell.

until I went there for the simple reason that I gave it credibility because I was number one, and we got some other number ones to come. I beat four number ones that day, and that sparked life into the whole circuit."

Once news of that tournament hit the magazines, the new names began to generate excitement once again. Tournament karate was breathing again. The great mass of karate fighters once again had role models, heroes, to emulate. It was like the old days, yet it wasn't. There were new faces, new styles, and more organization.

Vitali went on the road, traveling with his buddies Genova and Tucker and other notables such as Georgian Robert Harris, and a new type of point fighting style began to develop.

"I think because tournament karate had a few years to lie dormant, it gave us time to work and be innovative," Keith said. "Along with Genova and a few others in the South, we came up with a fighting style all our own. The idea was not to stand and take a shot to give a shot. We incorporated a lot of circular movement, a lot of angular techniques that mixed up other fighters. It was so new at the time that we took everybody off guard. Plus we had a lot of double kicks, the fake kicks, and they weren't prepared for that. Now, it's old hat to do a double kick or the type of movement we were doing in 1977–78.

"For example, the way we delivered a side kick—Genova and I figured it out from practical experience—that when you chamber your knee in the old traditional manner by bringing it straight up for the defensive side kick, it was too slow, it was not effective. We found that bringing your heel up in a straight line (toward the target), deleting that first step, cut the time in half, and your heel comes up in a direct line between you and your opponent. If nothing else, your opponent runs into that side kick. It proved to be the most essential technique in our arsenal."

Keith, Genova, and the others would swap ideas with, or learn techniques in action from, top fighters such as Ray McCallum, Dan Anderson, Nasty Anderson, Steve Fisher, John Longstreet. They were all new names on the circuit in 1978, but today they're household names for those who watch or participate in karate. These fighters assimilated the best of all techniques available, but perhaps it took a little longer to catch up with Keith and the innovative Southerners—long enough for Keith to be named the number one fighter in America for three straight years by not just one but several publications.

After winning the honor in 1980 Keith made a startling but brilliant move. He retired.

"We all had basically the same techniques, the same weapons,

Going Hollywood: Keith confronts a villain in a scene from *Revenge of the Ninja.*

in the top 10 anyway," he said. "Any one of them could have won on a given day; it just depended on who was 'on.' We had very tough fighters in McCallum and Nasty Anderson, and I said at the end of the third year it was time for me to leave because I wanted to leave on top like Bill Wallace. I wanted people to remember me as being the number one fighter when I left."

So many other athletes have failed to do that, resulting in

It's not all easy: Keith proves that being a star isn't always money, big cars, and fame. Sometimes it hurts.

untold damage to their futures. Keith's move worked to perfection. There was and is a great demand for the three-time national champion in a number of directions. He is still traveling monthly, sometimes weekly, to give seminars. He has made two movies, a bit part in *Force Five* and a costarring role in *Revenge of the Ninja*. He is an author. And he has a growing string of karate schools in Atlanta under his name but still within the Joe Corley

Playground action: In real life Keith Vitali would rather be out dancing than fighting, but movies have their own ideas.

system (loyalty is a strong Vitali trait). And there are calls and invitations from foreign countries—England, South America, Australia—asking him to visit on tour for seminars.

With all the distractions, fame, and money, Keith has stayed close to teaching and has been rewarded with tremendous results, turning out fighters like an assembly line. Among his students are nationally rated women, such as Stacey Duke and Rhonda Alex-

Teacher: Although he's one of tournament karate's greatest fighters, Keith Vitali still loves the teaching part of the sport.

ander, and men such as Vernon Johnson, plus up-and-coming fighters such as Jeff Farmer, Joe Navarro, Eddie Jones, Jerry Prince, Tony Young, and an even larger number of younger fighters who are still in the junior division. And unlike so many other "big names who only come around to count the money," Keith actually teaches his classes. Not only that, he gets in and spars and isn't worried about taking a shot from a student on occasion, saying it's a sign of good teaching. Whether or not he's joking about that, he's always praising, never negative.

He sounds almost too good to be true, but wherever you are when you read this—no matter what part of the country—you are within a phone call of verifying everything. Keith has friends wherever he's been who will praise him to high heaven.

Being a great fighter is one thing, but being a great person as well—that's hard to beat, and so is Keith Vitali.

Kent Mitchell

Index